for Beverly

changing weather

mark halperin

Mark Halperin
Ellensburg 2007

Cover and other paintings
by Bobbie Halperin

Some of these poems, at times in different form, first appeared in the following publications, which the author thankfully acknowledges:

Blue Mesa Review, "Deer-Hide" and "Three Properties of
　　Dutch Primitives"
Georgetown Review, "Memory"
Indiana Review, "The Fat Man" and "The Thin Man"
Kickass Review, "Leaves in the Wind"
NeoVictorian/Cochlea, "Jays to the Feeder"
Poems & Plays, "Impotence"
Prairie Schooner, "Death of Abraham," "Forbidden
　　Knowledge," and "Lot and His Daughters"
Smartish Pace, "Even Brahms"

Cover and other paintings by Bobbie Halperin

for B

EVEN BRAHMS

The throaty clarinet marches up
the stairs of a scale and you smile—
ruefully perhaps—but born along
by the simple flow of it, as if here
    an order of dignity existed
    that nowhere else existed—
    as if even Brahms knew

disappointment occurs so regularly
you could drown without music.
Even Brahms, bourgeois and so
uncouth that Tchaikovsky recalled
    his beery breath, rose to
    his toes when his turn came
    for the slow, quick-quick

and all the tucked in layers of thick
harmony. Suppose no one is worthy
of music's consolation and forgiveness
is always qualified. Suppose music
    is inherently weak, made up
    of disembodied yearning.
    Despite that thin source, its

fleeting nature, like smoke or lives
filled with disenchantment—isn't
music, meaning nothing itself,
expressiveness itself? Think of
     the play of wind on water,
     how it roars for instead of us,
     the clarinet as breathing space.

THREE PROPERTIES
OF DUTCH PRIMITIVES

When most people died young and there was no relief for pain, you'd think painters and their patrons would have favored serene scenes. Instead, one after another, you find magistrates flayed alive, and endlessly penetrated St. Sebastians. The numbers of the beheaded rival those of the watching horsemen. Before he's crucified, Christ is flailed and soldiers press down on the crown of thorns until blood flows. The loin-clothed saints are boiled, burned alive or have their limbs hacked off and their tongues docked. The perpetrators bear bestial faces that look as familiar as the street sweeper, the candle maker, the butcher.

Each toe is always distinct, perhaps because when they are painted, they belong chiefly to a Christ about to have his feet washed. Fingers are simply divided into two pairs plus a thumb. These belong to women at prayer, Marys and Barbaras, Annas and Catherines. Eyelids are oriental, curving like an "S" on its side. Artists like Van Der Wyden favor elongation. Their deposed Christs sag. Others treat the Virgin's face as a taut, inverted triangle, her chin a point from which the rising sides diverge. In place of mouths they paint small bows.

Landscapes disappear into blue-green at the farthest interior of pictures; sometimes this is sea, sometimes sky, dense or more dilute. After the 16th century, this color disappears along with emphatic perspective, proportion by significance, and faces that seem penciled in and lightly tinted. Blue becomes one color, green another, and their glassy melding melts away.

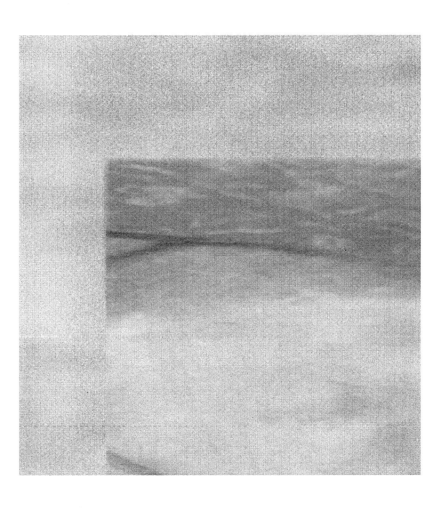

JAYS TO THE FEEDER

Here come the jays, two and three,
to swing at the feeder awkwardly,
iridescent as lightening bolts
with a blackish sheen to them, four and five
bouncing across the lawn. They arrive
cocks a mess, bobbing scolds

looking left to right then jumping up
a limb and up a limb to sup
on suet. For bravado's tacky sake
one back-wings the wind. Another
stabs the ground for seed-spill, hungrier
than his brothers. Now they're all aflutter and shake

their wings out to out-do that rising howl
they otherwise pay no mind to but travel
along, all puffed up and out
of order and fiercer than ice is or the blue
they collect and display as no more than their due,
paying back the raucousness they're all about.

THE DEATH OF ABRAHAM

When he first experiences the lilies, brooks, the balms,
oils, and wines of Paradise, Abraham
has no age. Lifted up, he is not dead,
although no longer on or of the earth. Instead,
the higher he ascends, the brighter it becomes;
he's arrayed in light; the gates and fountains, gemstones...

A child again among other children, he plays
their games, he sings their songs, he naps. When he awakes,
he's a young man, and strolls with others, to delight
in a visual clarity they never had in life.
Again, he rests. Again, he wakes, now an old man
sitting among his peers, discussing mercy and pardon.

God announces he's only seen the smallest part
of Paradise. In the Midrash, Abraham is smart
enough to know the cycle will go on and on.
Not simultaneous, but ages in succession—
the sages don't dismiss our wish to know with a sublime,
incomprehensible "time outside of time."

A tired Abraham requests of God an end,
though this time, he's the one who chooses. God assents
and Abraham expires. Those he leaves in Paradise,
beside its purling streams and myrrh, what do the wise
say of them or Abraham's soul? The Midrash tells
of a stone that hung around his neck, nothing else.

FORBIDDEN KNOWLEDGE

I.

When, after a few moments of standing, her arm
relaxed, nothing happened; she bit down. Juice ran
down her chin, apple-firm, pear-rich, pulpy as a plum.

She looked at grass, the far horizon. Clouds stacked,
one on another. She heard water, the trill of warblers.
Dread passed, replaced by an anticipation. Trees flickered.

The ripple across her skin, could be the pin-pricks of
time beginning between this one and the next. What
started up again? Each action points away, yet starts

from here—toward expectation? Bending to drink,
you trust the throat to swallow, the body to show the way.
Does fatigue lurk like a problem, or is that someone watching?

II.

I told her nothing. Why would we speak?
I reached around, behind, and looked
into her questioning face. That took
her by surprise. He knees grew weak.

She sank so slowly to the ground
she could have been a petal. Say
I told her that, as man held sway
over all creatures to be found

in Eden, so had I; he would
be replaced too—the last to come
rules the others. She understood,
wanted a moratorium,

an end to time and what it hid.
Did she push me away? Who
can be sure now? Maybe I whispered
in her ear. Maybe I licked it too.

And maybe all the stories show
is that their tellers mistrust snakes,
themselves and women. One mistakes
words for deeds, another, the glow

of satisfaction for deceit—
till you suspect they're jealous of
the two of us. And it's enough
that we lay down. Legends compete

for believers. Before there were words,
there were murmurs. Desire stirs
as dust does, as children clutch
at fingers. Before we hear, we touch.

He turned toward the center of the garden, stopped. Or I've invented that. She's disappeared. See her or see the tree behind her as if it moved and replaced her. She's gone. Where she'd been awakens, as from the dream she emerged from. If she can appear after sleeping, she can disappear while awake. After a step or two, there is a woman. She offers fruit. Can I go where she went? Leaves rustle, birdsong crosses birdsong, underneath, the clicking of crickets and grasshoppers: a wall of moving sound. She smiles. Nothing is familiar.

HOMAGE: PHOTOS

In one, Aunt Dunia and another aunt I never met stand on a barren road in Soviet Georgia. Neither woman smiles though their bodies turn toward each other and their arms link. In another, Mother, portions of her face a washed-out, featureless *terra incognito,* looks straight back, as if she knew what would develop, preferring to be seen this way. And Father's collage: amused, tab-collared shirt, tie not quite drawn tight to disguise his youth. He sports a soft brimmed fedora, or, coatless, straddles an "Indian" motorcycle. Always glasses, always a throat neatly shaved and vulnerable, hair parted on the left though he was right-handed. How clear eyed they appear. None will emerge from subway exits, none step through the sliding doors of airport terminals or woven, moon-cast shadows. Is it *oh no* or *good-bye* they're whispering so quietly you have to tip forward to hear?

DRUNK

When he called her to pick him up because
he was drunk at the AA or whatever they call
the sessions he had to attend after the drunk-
driving conviction, she swore this was the last
straw, the last time, and he swore he'd stop.
He'd been sad, he tried to explain... I know better

than to blame the sick for their illnesses and better
still how booze can soothe, maybe because
I've drunk past the point where I could stop
and took one sip more too often to recall
what came next. I should be the last
to judge. So if it's hard to say you're drunk—

and I know it is, even when you know you're drunk—
how much harder to admit you're better
off quitting? You almost tell yourself it's the last
time and then don't say the words because
saying them would make it public. You'll stop,
but, suppose... at that moment you recall

the wash of alcohol, its veil, like all
shades, muting and cooling, the pause when you've drunk
just enough. But if he doesn't stop,
if he gets in his car and kills someone, she'd better
not be married to him. We blame not because
we want to, but to save for ourselves a last

distance, and distinguish what cannot last
from what we can push away. As if all
that were needed was to call your bluff, "yours" because
"I" is too impersonal for the drunk
to show through. You figure, like any bettor,
take calculated chances. If I can't stop

thinking of him, as she can't stop
believing change is possible, his last
hope collapses ours and there's no better
or worse, just an end, memory's recall
failing like resolve or blame. Who's a drunk
to be a drunk? Who's excused because

of faulty recall or whatever out-lasts
it? Ask a drunk, but don't expect you'll stop
him drinking or that knowing makes you better.

PEREGRINE

It may be that even the slightest physical weakness or
difference in plumage can disastrously affect a bird's
ability to escape. Perhaps a sick bird does not wish to
live.   —ROBERT MACFARLANE

With a heightened consciousness of their fragility,
the weak work their way in like splinters, relishing
each small pleasures, each aggravation, free

to play on nerves like unoiled hinges. The peregrine
balances an energy checkbook: expend
less than you use; the gain is fat for when

pickings are scare or none and you become
like prey, weak and slow. It's all business.
Accountant or cutthroat, pity's not part of his
idiom, nor favors. Whatever you imagine is foreign

to that unhooded gaze. Who'd recognize
himself? Who'd manage to stare down or back
at those gold rimmed pupils? And his stoney attack,
dropping from the sky, is pure surprise.

LOT AND HIS DAUGHTERS

1.

Had it been revenge, to shame him
as he shamed us, offering to assuage
the men that day by sending us to them
instead of giving up his visitors—as
if his good name were worth ours—
had it been that, we could have waited
meekly for years to bring him low,
imagined him on his back or knees,
and we, swaying above, reminding him.
There wasn't time. Hate baits it hooks,
waits to hatch its schemes, while we,
compliant, ate our pride and took control.
We were alone—as young as he was
old. Who could endure the loneliness
his actions brought? Could you have
tilled the earth, listened to birds' song,
cooked meals and, humming, washed
the clothes and bathed? Each month
your blood would still cry out: un-
clean, your life would ebb a little more.
It's the voracious body that seeks out
its own gratifications, having learned
a declined language: hillock, furrow,
man and child. It needs to know.

2.

When an old man lies down there's no telling
if he'll wake or next to whom: in heaven, or hell
for that matter, the difference, at times, too small
to bother with. Take the dark, the way it shields
and yet invites. Better yet, keep your own council,
and let women think what they please. It's they
who'll pass the story on. In this game you move
and lose—either the dream or the startled partner
who was there. I can't say what I knew or felt.
There was the fogging wine. Velvety, opaque,
it stunned like flesh almost, in which we loose
self and inhibition, another pair, like you and who
you were. To move slowly, the way a lover does,
prolongs pleasure. To move slowly as travelers
in unknown country, on untested bridges, across
swamps, quicksand, starts another day: of trees
that seem new, new grass, new breath. An old man
counts: how many daughters do I have? Confused,
he starts again: how many did I have, or do I dream?

3.

An older sister should protect,
and once, when it was clear from what,
she always did. Someone forgot.
Someone was lost. Look at the plane, the prospect—
her figure on it, flat and dull
as matted grass. They feed that, fistful

by fistful to the baa-ing sheep,
belled and bawling, who run off when
they hear footsteps. The stink of them
is like yesterday. Forget sleep.
Forget escape. Think this could be
forever. She is small, pretty,

and would be shy if there were boys
to be shy with. The other, who could
be jealous, isn't. So the good
sister becomes mother, annoys,
telling her what to do, but less
than a longing she can't express,

and when that builds like gray rain-clouds
or hunger or the need to fall,
wide-eyed, arms open, sister's all
she has. Who leads, who pushes doubts
behind who? We know their order,
wine then sleep, one then the other.

MEMORY

Who could forget how memory betrays
first hours, months, then years, how it grows slack
then blanker, seems unfocused, grays

of dispersed wakes spreading an overlapping haze.
First in, last out, the classic "push-down stack"—
I had forgotten: memory betrays

memory. Near his end, my father's days
were all in Russian, as if he'd gone back
to the Black Sea, a framed and glazed

sepia photograph that's left no trace
as image bleeds into whatever fact
can be forgotten. Memory betrays

even its sources, unmooring place from place,
person from person. To the amnesiac,
all maps are creased and frayed, with grays

like turned off TV sets. My father's gaze
roamed wider, wilder, as if he'd lost track
even of time. Memory betrays
and is betrayed, its final grace.

DEER-HIDE

i.

On mornings when a branch blackens with massed
    ravens, I know why they are there,
and how they'll hold on until I'm too near
    to risk and flock back once I've passed.

Coming home, I'll slow down as I pass,
    check the bank and scan its steep
side, eyes raking the brush piles and drifts of deep
    leaves filled with shimmering bits of glass.

ii.

Next day, it's my wife who makes out the head
    and crumpled form. What she takes for
an immature bald eagle climbs, then soars
    above the river. It's the dead

that call and call to raven and crow, the rot
    of meat to feed on. They wait for
their carrion patiently. And sooner or later
    it appears, they eat and then it's not

their turn but the maggots' and ants', or, if it's still
    cold, mine. I'm last. I park my car.
I clamber down the shoulder and not far
    off, spot the unrecognizable

carcass, a jumble now of hair and bone.
    I cut strips from its hide for flies
to fool unwary trout this spring, my eyes,
    sailor-wise, on the wide horizon.

CHOICES

You make your choices and you live with them
like family, although one does not choose
one's family, and the past—whatever happened—

is immutable as histories or children
who start from us, but wander off, amused
by our odd choices. You live with them

like threatening voices, which, at times condemn
you, pitiless reminders one can lose
a family and a past. Whatever happened,

happened. Or does it happen over again
into infinity? You could confuse
choice with loss, but have to live with them

both, compelled to, although no one will listen
to protests. Plan away. It's no use.
Your familiar past might never have happened.
It fades like choices and lives that could have been.

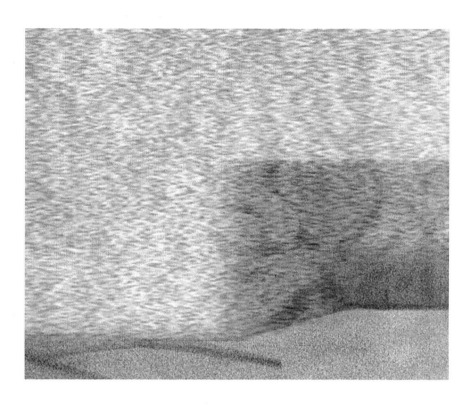

LEAVES IN THE WIND

There's a whistle inside the rumble of traffic
and thickly needled pines, a metallic clicking
in the lilacs, the shrieks of hawks, dogs barking,

woodpeckers tapping, snapping sheets, a quiet
that seems to drag the few unfallen leaves.
They curl, pinned like brittle yellow and orange

and red hair-bows, rustle, shaken by the thin
branches they hang and move away from,
inhaling wind, expanding. They're done

accomplishing something steely and chilly
as drum-rolls, a thrumming, and almost as
noiselessly as turning pages replace each other.

IMPOTENCE

The impotent man is of two minds,
upper and lower. One is full
    of desire; the other passes.
    In practice, this means he finds
himself stripped for action, unable
to achieve his ends, lower half,

half or less than what's needed, spineless,
not up to the task at hand. The head
    sees things that way. Below,
    what's going on is less
clear. Do you need to think in bed,
to ponder there too? Yes and No.

Divided loyalties, failures of nerve,
remind us that we're free enough
    to be absurd, and at
    the worst moments. Serve,
says Spirit, but Flesh replies: tough
luck. It can't or won't. That's that—

the impotent man's all done,
maybe forever, limp with dejection,
    red faced, but not
    hot enough to begin.
If a pensive cock's an oxymoron,
what about substantiated thought?

insight incarnadine? a gun
squinting? Imagine whatever winds
    your clock, then try on his mood
    slipping from bed. Someone's
gone off and not gone off. Mind
mirrors matter. The body broods.

IN ODESSA

In Odessa wrist-thick grape vines climb and shade the
    walls of the stone buildings with plump leaves,
the elegant old Opera and Ballet Theatre undergoes
    "remont,"
and azure dumpsters are rummaged through several
    times an hour—
Odessa of tree lined Pushkinskaya and Richelevskaya
    streets my father walked,
who would have thought I'd walk,
and Grecheskaya (Greek) and Ekaterininskaya
    (Catherine) too,
guessed I'd live between Evreiskaya (Jewish), and
    Troitskaya (Trinity), the old KGB building, my
    neighbor,
or imagined my conversations, "where are you from,"
    recognizing the inflection,
or that I'd track down the phone number of one possible
    remaining distant cousin, call,
and the lack of interest in the dull voice of the woman
    who answered?

I'll leave off tripping over the raised paving stones soon
    enough,
shuffling through old postcards at the flea-market in the
    Maldavanka,
pestering Boris, who brought me to see the shiny new
    storefronts at Starokonny Rinok (the Old-horse
    Market),
and lingering over the Korean carrot salad in Privoz
    market, attentive for the pickpockets I've been
    warned of.
I'm refilling two plastic five-liter bottles with water for
    cooking at one of the taps of the public well,
carrying them back up my four flights
and stand at the kitchen window
and look out over the rooftops, past the harbor derricks,
further than the dots of distant ships, below the shifting
    surface of the Black Sea
to its oxygen-less crypt, where nothing decays.

FOR JIM SPOTTS
d. 2004

What was it you got wrong like love
you could not give? The morning that you eyed
  your steaming plate of grits
in a road-side café and said with pride
  you could make anyone like you, as if
  you thought I'd envy such a gift,

I let it pass. It was fall and you
driving us to some fishing hole. What strikes
  me now is how I tagged along, content
to be with someone I'd never met the likes
  of. Your surprise must have been   ·
  as improbable as our friendship then.

In the cabin I'd drive four hours to
where you surfaced after your divorce, you'd boast
  of luck with women, work, and let
the brandy settle over us. We'd lost
  touch though, and whatever we had had,
  had passed, leaving gaps instead.

Even loss flows till there's nothing
left to tell you what you miss. The bigger fish,
  the better cast, who drove who home...
Rest, my competitive friend. No one would wish
  to die the way as you did: a brief
  gasp, unable to believe

28

the end has come in an empty field.
Someone heard the dog barking above
your lifeless body. We're alone
too much, too often to call death's bluff,
and grow too tired or private to stray.
Who would we talk to, what would we say?

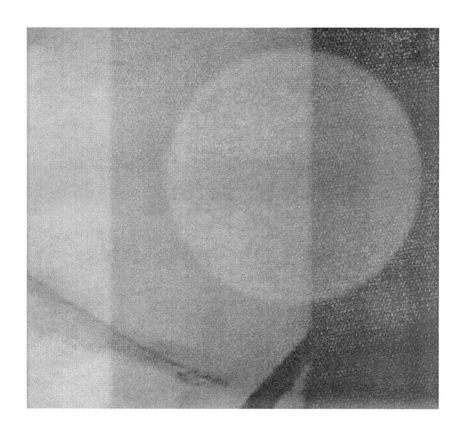

POUSSIN

Even when a storm is brewing in Poussin
the surfaces of ponds retain a calm, unbroken blue,
and robes, primary greens and reds and yellows, worn
by the main figures, spread left and right, anchoring the view,

balancing without repeating. Plains climb, divide—
buildings shrink, then whiten, puffing like stalled clouds,
which rise but seem never to have moved, as stiff

as linen, just as the figures seem, less caught than bound—
aloof, not frozen—insular, detached. As if
there were no time or what there was remained outside

the changing weather, and passion couldn't carry
you off like faint bells or smells, a puff
or pulse. As if Poussin had never lived
among us, the gray, noisy and ordinary.

A NEW TOWN

How easy getting lost is,
not so much in a fog as

among constant distractions,
beacons, appeals. The eye numbs,

stunned by a fence, each paling
topped with a turret, the sting

of car fumes and sea salt—views,
horizons. If you could choose

to, you'd choose to misread signs,
landmarks, take the road that climbs

still higher, but by day three
you automatically

turn right at the right corner,
not looking up to check for

the street, slip in the unsigned
entrance to your courtyard, find

you've climbed the stairs, fished out
your key and stand there about

to twist it in the lock, not

having thought where your route

led, attention waning, on
auto-pilot, as often

fading in as out, ahead
as behind yourself. You dread

what is coming, even as
now, turning the knob, you pause.